Step onto Main Street, U.S.A. and suddenly the stress of contemporary life gives way to the quaint and reassuring charms of turn-of- the-century America. Time seems to slow and soften amid the smells of freshly baked muffins and candies, the steady clip-clop of the horse-drawn streetcar, and the twinkling pin-lights outlining the gingerbread trim of the buildings. It is the essence of the hometown America that greeted the dawn of the 20th century.

Main Street, U.S.A.

The hub of all Main Street transportation can be found in Town Square. From here guests can travel in style up Main Street in an open-air Horse-Drawn Streetcar, Main Street Fire Engine, Horseless Carriage, or double-decker Omnibus. At the Main Street Station the four authentic steam trains of the Disneyland® Railroad take guests on a grand circle tour of the Magic Kingdom. During the excursion, guests travel along the rim of the Grand Canyon and journey through the incredible Primeval World.

On Main Street, U.S.A. a variety of dining pleasures awaits. From the simple delight of pickles in the Market House, to the freshly baked goods of the Blue Ribbon Bakery, to the fanciful creations of the Gibson Girl Ice Cream Parlor, to the patio dining of the Carnation Café, to the Victorian splendor of the Plaza Inn—guests are sure to find something to satisfy the most discriminating of tastes.

The popular animated windows of the Emporium and the mouthwatering sights behind the windows of the Candy Palace and Candy Kitchen help make Main Street, U.S.A. a window-shopper's paradise. Along Main Street you can easily find the perfect gift or souvenir—from traditional Mickey Mouse "ears" and Disney collectibles of the past to fanciful silhouettes made while you wait.

The harmonies of the Dapper Dans (the resident barbershop quartet of Main Street) and the oomp-pa-pa of the Disneyland® Marching Band are always present to serenade guests with their turn-of-the-century musical repertoire. Guests on Main Street can also find nostalgic entertainment in the vintage black and white Mickey Mouse films of the Main Street Cinema and the silent "flickers" of the hand-cranked movieolas of the Penny Arcade. Daily parades and the traditional flag-lowering ceremony contribute to the Main Street hometown atmosphere.

The Walt Disney Story Featuring Great Moments with Mr. Lincoln is an inspiring salute to Walt Disney, his pioneering career, and his admiration for the wisdom and achievements of Abraham Lincoln. The show features a display of much of Walt Disney's personal correspondence, early archival photos, and exacting replicas of Disney's two studio offices. The stirring presentation of Great Moments with Mr. Lincoln incorporates actual photographs from the Civil War and one of the most advanced examples of Audio-Animatronics® technology.

In Adventureland your senses are stirred by the sights of lush jungle foliage, the sounds of wild animals, and the aromas of tropical blossoms. This realm of adventure and exploration is an amazing amalgam of many of the world's far-off places and uncharted regions. One quick turn can lead to the hot sands of the Middle East (Aladdin's Oasis), the tropical magic of Polynesia (Walt Disney's Enchanted Tiki Room), the vastness of Africa (Tarzan's Treehouse™), the exotic rivers of the world (Jungle Cruise), or the steamy jungles of Asia (Indiana Jones™ Adventure).

Adventureland

Join Professor Jones deep in the heart of Asia for the Indiana Jones™ Adventure. It's 1935 and discovery awaits in the Temple of the Forbidden Eye. Brave guests board well-worn troop transports that take them into a strange, subterranean world where they have an unfortunate encounter with the mysterious temple deity Mara in the great Chamber of Destiny. Forced to flee, guests narrowly escape a collapsing bridge, giant snakes, thousands of rats, booby-traps, and the prospect of being crushed by a 5-ton boulder!

Cross over a rickety suspension bridge to Tarzan's Treehouse™, which celebrates the high-flying escapades of the "Lord of the Apes." Based on the hit Disney animated film *Tarzan*®, this climb-through adventure 70-feet above Adventureland allows guests to scale Tarzan™'s treetop home and relive many of the film's exciting and memorable moments. At the base of the tree, kids can "trash the camp" in an interactive area filled with shipwreck supplies. Occasionally, live animals and well-known characters like Tarzan™, Jane, and even the rambunctious gorilla Terk greet guests as they exit the treehouse.

The Jungle Cruise has hosted millions of would-be explorers aboard its thrilling excursions into the jungle. From the safety of your launch, witness the gathering of animals on the African Veldt or perhaps catch a rare glimpse of the "Lost Safari," a group of unfortunate adventurers who always seem to be in the company of an angry rhino.

Walt Disney's Enchanted Tiki Room entertains Adventureland guests with its irreverent presentation in which "the birdies sing and the flowers croon." The macaw hosts of the show—José, Michael, Fritz, and Pierre—have welcomed hundreds of thousands of guests into their special "world of joyous songs and wondrous miracles."

Over 225 birds, flowers, and tikis delight the audience with the melodious Enchanted Fountain, some Offenbach, and a rousing rendition of "Let's All Sing Like the Birdies Sing." According to the birds, their show is designed to "fill you with pleasure and glee because if we don't make you feel like that, we're gonna wind up on a lady's hat!"

The breathtaking sight of the gleaming white Mark Twain Riverboat or the imposing gallantry of the Columbia Sailing Ship as it approaches the dock beckons guests into Frontierland, a robust panorama of America's pioneer past. As soon as you pass through the stockade entrance you are surrounded by an amalgam of sights and sounds that authentically conjures up images from America's western expansion, from the bustling riverfronts of the Mississippi and Missouri Rivers of the late 1700s to the dusty southwestern desert of the 1880s.

FOWLER'S INN

The Rivers of America in Frontierland provides a variety of ways for would-be pioneers of all ages to explore the wilderness outposts of the backwoods. The dazzling white Mark Twain Riverboat carries guests upriver in southern elegance, while the 84-foot-tall, 10-gun, three-masted Columbia Sailing Ship lets passengers relive life aboard an authentic replica of the first American ship to sail around the world. Guests can get a close-up look at river life from one of the authentic Mike Fink Keel Boats as they navigate the backwaters of the Rivers of America.

Big Thunder Mountain Railroad—"the wildest ride in the wilderness!"—whisks brave guests back to the Gold Rush era. Hop aboard runaway mine trains and race around towering buttes, dive into dangerous gulches, and plunge deep into foreboding caverns filled with bats and phosphorescent pools. The reckless trains careen past raging waterfalls, splash through still waters, and finally encounter a deafening earthquake from which the mountain gets its name.

TETTER-TOTTER ROCK
GIANT PUNCH BOWL
AMBUSH ROCK

Log rafts transport guests across the Rivers of America to Tom Sawyer Island, an oasis of adventure where kids of all ages can follow in the footsteps of Tom, Huck Finn, and Becky Thatcher. Guests can explore the foreboding Injun Joe's Cave, rock and sway across Suspension Bridge, splash across Barrel Bridge, or keep a lookout for river pirates from the sentry posts of Fort Wilderness.

On select nights the Rivers of America in Frontierland erupts into the nighttime spectacular FANTASMIC! One of the most complex and technically advanced shows ever presented at Disneyland® Park, this hugely popular extravaganza features a battle of good and evil inside Mickey Mouse's fanciful imagination, highlighting scenes from Disney's animated classics including *Fantasia*, *Peter Pan*, *Beauty and the Beast*, and *Sleeping Beauty*.

Here is the Paris of the American frontier, the Crescent City of New Orleans as it was 150 years ago. Within its sheltered courtyards and winding streets, elegance and charm mingle comfortably with the almost constant and irreverent sounds of Dixieland jazz. Under its ornate wrought-iron balconies are some of the most distinctive restaurants and shops in Disneyland® Park. This bend of the river also plays host to two signature Disneyland attractions—Pirates of the Caribbean and the Haunted Mansion.

New Orleans Square

"Set sail with the wildest crew that ever sacked the Spanish Main" aboard the high-seas adventure Pirates of the Caribbean. You'll encounter fun-loving rogues in search of treasure, but be warned that "Dead Men Tell No Tales." From the mysterious grottos of Davy Jones' Locker to the rambunctious buccaneers plundering a seaport village, Pirates of the Caribbean is a memorable adventure for seafarers of all ages.

"Welcome foolish mortals to the Haunted Mansion," home to 999 frightfully funny ghosts and happy haunts— but there is always room for one more! There is no shortage of hot- and cold-running chills in this stately antebellum mansion— each room is furnished with wall-to-wall creaks. All the spirits are "just dying to meet you" as you tour the house in your own private "Doom Buggy." But beware of hitchhiking ghosts—they just may try to follow you home!

Under an umbrella of constant midnight sky in the Blue Bayou Restaurant, hearty appetites can enjoy the restaurant's famous Monte Cristo sandwiches. The Blue Bayou's romantic moonlit dining can be enjoyed all day long accompanied by the sight of an occasional shooting star and dancing fireflies.

Located above the Pirates of the Caribbean adventure, The Disney Gallery serves as a showcase for the artwork of Walt Disney Imagineering. Here guests can buy original or limited-edition images of Disneyland attraction designs, posters, and concept art. Throughout the year the Gallery hosts a series of events and art signings, many of them featuring some of the original Disney Imagineers who helped to create the park.

As guests enter New Orleans Square they encounter Port d'Orleans, a lively mart that features items imported directly from Louisiana, such as a variety of spicy Cajun sauces, beignet mixes, and coffees with chicory. Within New Orleans Square guests can also discover one-of-a-kind pieces of estate jewelry, have customized parasols decorated, or have their portrait rendered in pastels.

Nestled in a lazy corner of the backwoods is Critter Country. Here amid shady trees and cool streams is a world where the rabbits, bears, opossums, foxes, alligators, owls, and frogs are just as social and neighborly as they can be. Keen eyes might spot wily Brer Rabbit outsmarting Brer Fox and Brer Bear atop Chickapin Hill. And keen ears will surely catch the applause and laughter drifting from the world-famous Country Bear Playhouse.

Critter Country

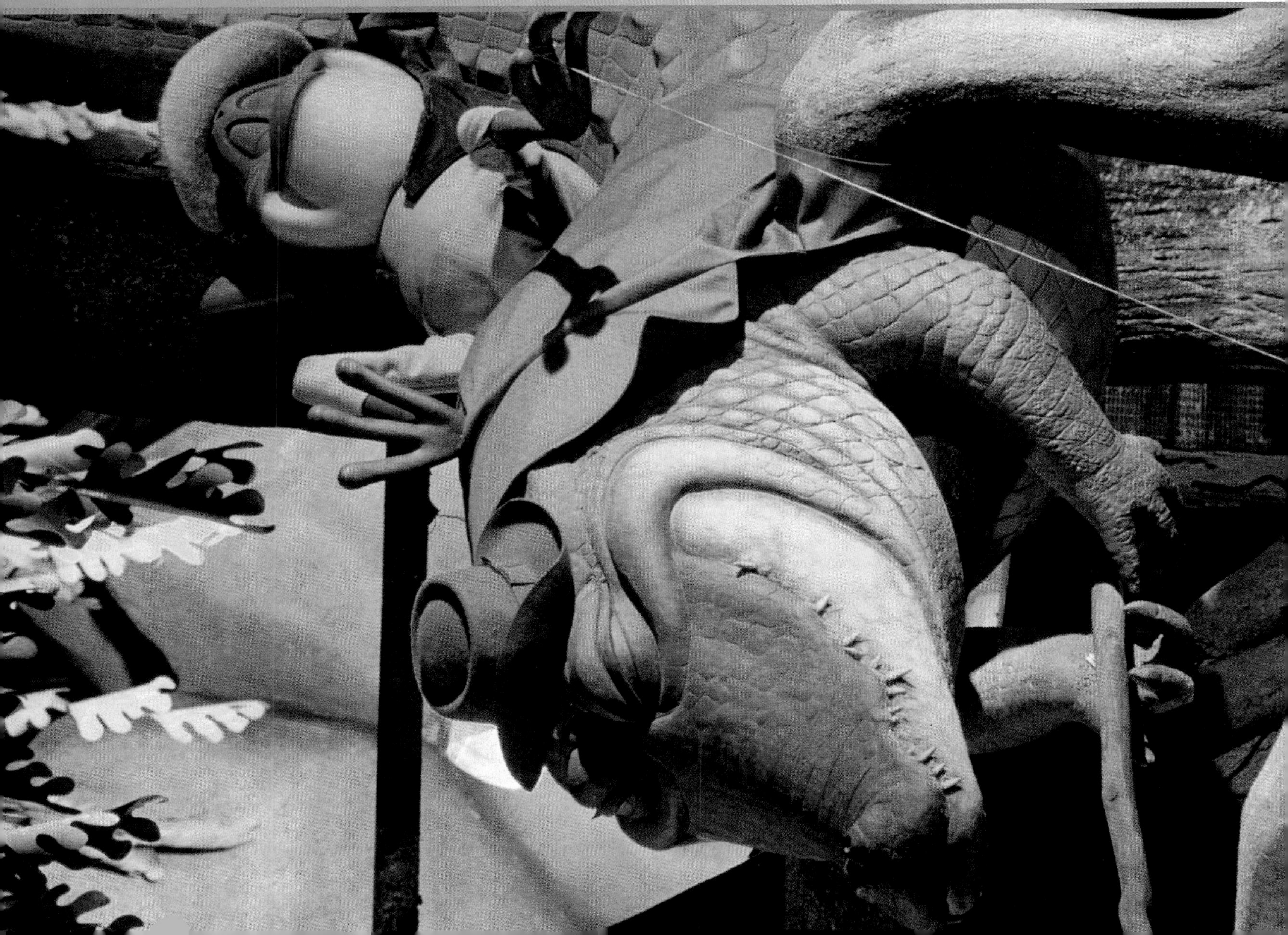

The Country Bear Playhouse is home to a cast of bruins not seen in your typical national park. Nobody hibernates through the rollicking, foot-stomping, paw-pounding country-western musical antics of the bodacious Five Bear Rugs, the swinging Teddi Barra, and the sorrowful heart tugging refrains of Big Al. The show changes seasonally and includes performances of The Country Bear Christmas Special and The Country Bear Vacation Hoedown.

Every day is a "Zip-a-Dee-Doo-Dah" kind of day in Critter Country. Here you can savor long lazy afternoons in the shade or simply delight in the rustic country atmosphere. Enjoy down-home dining at the Hungry Bear Restaurant along the river's edge or quench your thirst in the Brer Bar. At the Briar Patch, you can find items suitable to decorate any den, cave, or home.

Hop aboard one of Davy Crockett's Explorer Canoes for an exciting paddle-powered excursion around the Rivers of America. Crashing through the wake of the mighty *Mark Twain* and a thrilling encounter with an authentic encampment of Plains Indians along the riverbank are only part of the adventure in this hands-on exploration of the frontier.

Inspired by the classic Disney film *Song of the South* and the wise fables of Uncle Remus, Splash Mountain provides brave guests with a chance to follow in the perilous footsteps of wily Brer Rabbit. Search for your "Laughing Place" as you journey through this exciting flume adventure featuring five drops, including a hair-raising finale that sends you on a 52-foot, 45° angle, 40-mph plunge into a watery briar patch.

Cross over the moat and through the archways of Sleeping Beauty Castle to enter "the happiest kingdom of them all"—Fantasyland. Enchanted tales of childhood adapted from classic Disney animated films come to life in this timeless realm of imagination. Within the magical Old World setting guests can fly through the London night to Never Land, see an elephant fly, take a spin in a giant teacup, and brave the icy thrills of the Matterhorn.

Fantasyland

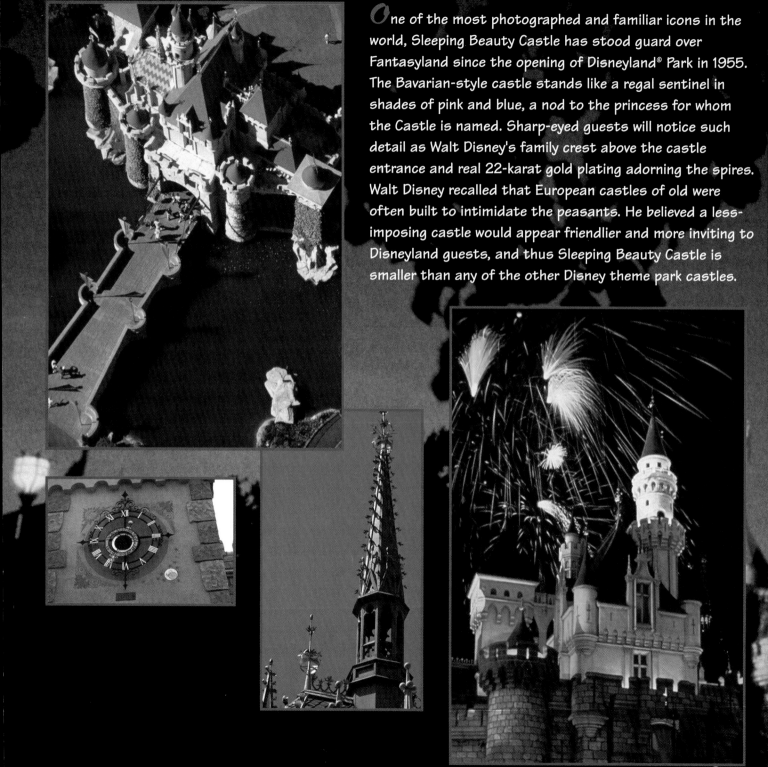

One of the most photographed and familiar icons in the world, Sleeping Beauty Castle has stood guard over Fantasyland since the opening of Disneyland® Park in 1955. The Bavarian-style castle stands like a regal sentinel in shades of pink and blue, a nod to the princess for whom the Castle is named. Sharp-eyed guests will notice such detail as Walt Disney's family crest above the castle entrance and real 22-karat gold plating adorning the spires. Walt Disney recalled that European castles of old were often built to intimidate the peasants. He believed a less-imposing castle would appear friendlier and more inviting to Disneyland guests, and thus Sleeping Beauty Castle is smaller than any of the other Disney theme park castles.

ℰnter Peter Pan's Flight and step aboard your own flying pirate galleon to sail through the Darling nursery and out over London. Follow Tinker Bell toward the "second star to the right" and straight on to Never Land. Passing amid twinkling stars you'll look down to spy such Never Land locales as Mermaid Lagoon and Skull Rock. After a harrowing encounter with the villainous Captain Hook, you'll join Peter Pan, Wendy, Michael, John, and Tinker Bell as their pixie-dusted galleon sails into the evening sky.

*P*inocchio's Daring Journey is sure to captivate with its well-loved story of the lonely woodcarver Geppetto and his desire to have a real son. Along cobblestone alpine roads, guests follow little Pinocchio and his faithful conscience Jiminy Cricket as they attempt to avoid fateful encounters with the wily Foulfellow and Gideon, the Coachman, and Monstro the Whale. Guided by the "wishing star," guests meet the lovely Blue Fairy and ultimately share in Pinocchio's happy ending.

*S*ite of numerous wedding proposals, the Snow White Wishing Well and Grotto provides a tranquil and romantic setting along the east side of the Sleeping Beauty Castle moat. The marble figures of Snow White and the Seven Dwarfs were a gift to Walt Disney from an Italian sculptor. Sharp-eared guests can hear Snow White's plaintive refrain of "I'm Wishing" echoing in the depths of the well.

*J*oin madcap adventurer J. Thaddeus Toad inside stately Toad Hall as he test drives his all-new motorcar and takes everyone on a "wild ride" across the English countryside and to "Nowhere in Particular." This is one of the most beloved Fantasyland attractions, where guests can race, leap, and crash their way through Mr. Toad's trials and tribulations.

*G*uests who venture on Snow White's Scary Adventures enter a timeless tale of romance. Here the lovable Seven Dwarfs celebrate with a "Silly Song" and the evil Queen transforms herself into a villainous Witch and offers Snow White a juicy apple laced with "the sleeping death." With the arrival of the Prince and love's first kiss, everyone lives happily ever after.

Don't be late for a very important date! Board your very own private Caterpillar and journey down the rabbit hole to join little Alice on her marvelous adventures. Unique to Disneyland® Park, the Alice in Wonderland adventure is filled with memorable characters and scenes such as the Unbirthday Party, Tweedle Dum and Tweedle Dee, the Garden of Flowers, and the March of the Cards. You can even join in a fateful round of croquet with the ever-explosive Queen of Hearts.

*A*board the Mad Tea Party guests can spin and spin and spin their cup and saucer in any direction in this life-size Unbirthday Party. With colorful Chinese paper lanterns hanging overhead and the familiar strains of the "Unbirthday Song" in the air, guests will surely feel as if they stepped right out of the memorable Disney film or the beloved storybook.

Secure in their various cages, boxcars, and cabooses, guests aboard the Casey Jr. Circus Train will cheer along as Casey proclaims "I think I can, I think I can, I think I can" while he chugs and puffs his way through the hills and valleys of Storybook Land.

STORYBOOK LAND

*A*board the colorful Storybook Land Canal Boats, each one named after a particular Disney character, guests glide gently past miniature homes and settings from some of Disney's most beloved characters and animated films including Geppetto's Village, Prince Eric's Castle, the Dwarfs' Diamond Mine, and Aladdin's city of Agrabah. Created at one-inch-to-one-foot scale, the intricately detailed dwellings are complemented by actual living miniature shrubs, flowers, and trees.

Guests have been captivated by "It's a Small World" since it first premiered at the park in 1966. A salute to the children of the world, this delightful attraction speaks the international language of goodwill. Its impressive exterior playfully represents landmarks from around the world including France's Eiffel Tower, Italy's Leaning Tower of Pisa, and India's famed Taj Mahal. Aboard their boats, guests journey beyond the Topiary Garden and drift with the tide into "The Happiest Cruise That Ever Sailed."

During the winter, the venerable attraction is transformed into the spectacular "it's a small world" Holiday, where the holiday traditions of many nations are fancifully displayed and the famous attraction score has been beautifully integrated with such seasonal favorites as "Deck the Halls" and "Jingle Bells."

*S*oar high over Fantasyland aboard Dumbo the Flying Elephant, the world's most famous flying pachyderm. A well-known European manufacturer of circus organs built the attraction's vintage mechanical band; the organ, built circa 1915, weighs three-quarters of a ton. Its circus-like music can be heard over a mile away.

The glittering King Arthur Carrousel beckons guests through the archway of Sleeping Beauty Castle. The classic carrousel horses are 90 to 110 years old and are hand-carved and hand-painted; no two are exactly alike. The turntable for the carrousel was made around 1875 and came from Canada. Most of the 19th-century horses were hand-carved in Germany.

owering 14 stories above Fantasyland, the snow-capped Matterhorn (a 1/100 scale replica of its Swiss namesake) is the breathtaking setting for a thrilling race through ominous ice caves and a frightening chance encounter with the Abominable Snowman. Waterfalls thunder down its icy slopes, which also feature Alpine forests and tranquil ponds. Occasionally, guests may spot Mickey and friends scaling the north face of the mountain.

DOWNTOWN TOONTOWN

FIVE ⬦ DIME

Bursting with color and frenetic energy, Mickey's Toontown is a 1930s classic Disney cartoon come to wacky life. Here in this "toon" social hub, animated stars such as Mickey Mouse, Minnie Mouse, Donald Duck, Goofy, Chip 'n' Dale, and Roger Rabbit live, work, and play, much to the delight of guests of all ages. From the bustle of its downtown to the charm of its residential neighborhood, Mickey's Toontown is a slice of "reel" life where virtually everything has a unique character and personality.

The welcome mat is always out at Mickey's House and Meet Mickey. Inside the California bungalow home guests can see where Mickey unwinds and view mementos of his famed career. Mickey himself is at work on a new film project in Mickey's Movie Barn out back. Guests are welcome to drop in to say hello and browse through the collection of props from some of his most famous film roles.

Minnie's House is painted in romantic hues of lavendar and pink, and is cozily situated right next door to Mickey's. Inside Minnie's House, guests can play with her computerized vanity, bang out a tune on her pots and pans in the kitchen, or assist her with baking a cake for Mickey. Outside guests can see her colorful garden and make a wish in her charming wishing well.

The bright red and gold-trimmed Jolly Trolley provides a rambling two-way trip to all of Mickey's Toontown, winding around Roger Rabbit's fountain in Downtown Toontown, traveling into Mickey's Neighborhood, and circling Mickey's fountain. A large gold wind-up key on top of the engine turns as the trolley runs, and a Tooned-up chassis gives the trolley an ambling, cartoon-like gait.

Inside Goofy's Bounce House kids can literally bounce right off the walls. This wacky home has a floor with just a little extra "cush" and the sofa is so fluffy that it can give little guests a lift! After seeing the instability of the inside, guests can easily understand why from the outside Goofy's Bounce House looks like it just might bounce off its foundation.

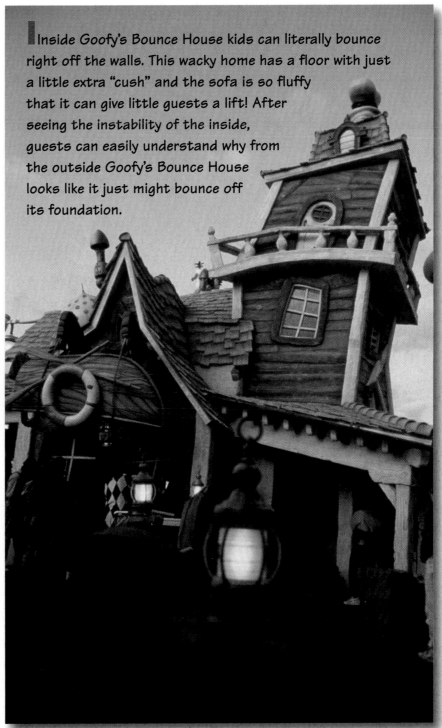

Gadget's Go-Coaster, located next to Donald's Boat on Toon Lake, is a high-speed, splash-down contraption for children of all ages. Made from what appear to be large spools, springs, rubber bands, and other assorted household goods, this little coaster is sure to give guests to Mickey's Toontown a beautiful view along with a few butterflies in their stomachs.

Aboard Roger Rabbit's Car Toon Spin guests ride along with Lenny the Cab as Roger tries to save his lovely Jessica from the dastardly Weasels and a fateful plunge in the deadly "Dip." On this twirling and whirling adventure, guests take a wacky trip through cartoon back alleys in their quest to avoid the Dip and save Jessica and all the citizens of Toontown.

Crossover into Tomorrowland and embark on an exciting journey into "Imagination and Beyond." This intriguing realm of imagination, discovery, and wonder was inspired by such classic futurists as Jules Verne, H.G. Wells, and Leonardo da Vinci, along with modern visionaries like George Lucas and Walt Disney. With its whirling spaceships, zooming rocket vehicles, lush vegetation, and kinetic sculptures and fountains Tomorrowland is an exciting look beyond the stars to a future full of promise and hope.

Tomorrowland

Pilot your own spaceship aboard the Astro Orbiter and soar through a fantastic, animated "astronomical model" of planets and constellations. With its colorful rockets circling a series of moving planets, the Astro Orbiter is a radiant and impressive kaleidoscope of colors in tones of burnished copper and brass.

You may have a change of perspective in the hilarious 3-D film experience Honey, I Shrunk the Audience. All seems well when Professor Wayne Szalinski is presented with the "Inventor of the Year" award from the Imagination Institute. But things go a bit awry when one of his inventions ultimately "shrinks" the audience.

Tomorrowland's landmark Carousel Theater, which previously housed the former Carousel of Progress and America Sings attractions, is now home to Innoventions. This two-level interactive pavilion of near-future technology brings the building's original concept into the high-tech world of today.

Innoventions features concepts and technology from the world's leading industries, and is divided into five main sections: Home, Entertainment, Workplace, Sports/Recreation, and Transportation. The interactive section of the attraction includes presentations and hands-on displays showcasing creative uses of tomorrow's technology. Guests then flow to a center atrium where they ascend to the upper-level concept presentations, all clustered around a striking illuminating tree that is literally "wired" for the future.

Towering above Tomorrowland is Observatron, a colorful kinetic sculpture representing the imaginative world of tomorrow and beyond. Sitting majestically atop the Rocket Rods loading platform, Observatron signals the quarter hour with an impressive array of movements, lights, and vibrant music. Under the Observatron is the official Disneyland home of Radio Disney. Through soundproof glass, guests can view Radio Disney's state-of-the-art radio studio and watch daily live broadcasts carried across the nation on "the radio network just for kids."

The Rocket Rods zoom above, through, and around Tomorrowland in the fastest and longest attraction in Disneyland® Park. This thrilling experience puts guests behind the wheels of high-speed vehicles of the future as they tear along an elevated highway above Tomorrowland.

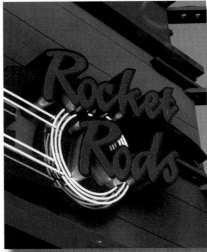

Under its metallic spires of green and copper, Space Mountain guests roar through deep space in a thrilling, high-speed adventure. Featuring an energetic and heart-pounding on-board soundtrack, this out-of-this-world journey whisks guests through the darkness of space, racing past giant meteors and shooting stars, and culminating in a hair-raising

Inside Star Tours guests experience a bustling intergalactic travel agency and spaceport where they soon find themselves aboard a StarSpeeder 3000 on a perilous journey to the moon of Endor. Based on George Lucas's famed film series, Star Tours is a harrowing trip through the cosmos, guided by Rex (a rookie pilot), R2D2, and C3PO. Along the way passengers survive a wild trip through an asteroid, narrowly escape an intergalactic dogfight, and successfully maneuver through the dangerous chasms of a Death Star.